Talking to My Body

ANNA SWIR

Talking to My Body

TRANSLATED BY CZESŁAW MIŁOSZ & LEONARD NATHAN

COPPER CANYON PRESS

Publication of this book is supported by a grant from the National Endowment for the Arts and a grant from the Lannan Foundation. Additional support to Copper Canyon Press has been provided by the Andrew W. Mellon Foundation, the Lila Wallace–Reader's Digest Fund, and the Washington State Arts Commission. Copper Canyon Press is in residence with Centrum at Fort Worden State Park.

Library of Congress Cataloging-in-Publication Data
Swirszczynska, Anna.
Talking to my body / Anna Swir : translated by Czeslaw Milosz and Leonard Nathan.
p. cm.
ISBN 1-55659-108-X
1. Swirszczynska, Anna – Translations into English.   1. Title.
PG7178.W57A25 1996
091.8'517 – dc20   96-10015

COPPER CANYON PRESS
P.O. BOX 271, PORT TOWNSEND, WASHINGTON 98368

Contents

39 *Wind*

55 *To Be a Woman*

Talking to My Body

Introduction

ANNA SWIR (SWIRSZCZYŃSKA) was born in Warsaw in 1909, the daughter of a painter. As she herself says, she literally grew up in her father's workshop, sleeping and preparing her lessons there. The poverty in which the family lived forced her to look for work early in life. In her own words: "I was then terribly shy, ugly, and crushed by a mountain of complexes." She put herself through university, studying medieval and baroque Polish literature and discovering the Polish language of the fifteenth century, which according to her, is the most vigorous. Her first poems, published in the 1930s, bear the marks both of her upbringing in the artistic milieu (images taken from paintings and albums of reproductions) and of her fascination with the Middle Ages. These are mostly short poems in prose, sophisticated miniatures, from which any personal accents are carefully eliminated. The form of the miniature was to return later, while the reticence about her personal life was to disappear.

The experience of war radically changed Anna. She shared the fate of Warsaw, beginning with the siege by the Nazis in September 1939, continuing through the years of the occupation, and ending with the final destruction of the city in the fall of 1944. A member of the Resistance, she wrote for underground publications. During the sixty-three days of the Warsaw Uprising in August-September 1944, she was a military nurse in an improvised hospital. A survivor – once she waited for an hour expecting to be executed – she says: "War made me another person. Only then did my own life and the life of my contemporaries enter my poems." However, as she confesses, she had great difficulty finding a proper form for what she had seen and lived through. Thirty years had to elapse before she succeeded in writing a volume of short poem-pictures on the Warsaw Uprising, *Building the Barricade* (1974). The technique of the miniature she elaborated in her youth now served a different purpose.

No less slow was her maturing as the poet of the present volume, primarily a poet of personal life, of love and love's pain. For several years she was known mostly as the author of poems and stories for children. Her volumes, straightforward in their sensuality, *Wind* (1970), *I Am A Woman* (1972) and *Happy As A Dog's Tail* (1978) indicate that she started to tackle the subject of eroticism only in her sixties. In them she is also an outspoken feminist.

The central theme of her mature poems is flesh. Flesh in love-ecstasy, flesh in pain, flesh in terror, flesh afraid of loneliness, exuberant, running, lazy, flesh of a woman giving birth, resting, snoring, doing her morning calisthenics, feeling the flow of time or reducing time to one instant. By such a clear delineation of her subject matter, Anna Swir achieves in her sensual and fierce poetry a nearly calligraphic neatness.

I have wondered why the poems of Anna Swir's that I have read aloud in translation were so liked by American audiences. Among the many women poets in America there are several who write about a woman's body with a directness similar to hers, and yet the listeners distinguished in her a new tone, of rare intensity. The difference is, I believe, that she is more objective than her American contemporaries, because the body, including her own, is for her both the subject of perceptions and an object observed with detachment. "If people find her poems appealing, why don't you translate more of them and make a book?" asked a friend of mine. His suggestion, however, would not have been enough to prompt me, if not for a special dimension I discovered in these poems' very earthiness.

During our century various kinds of language traditionally used to cope with our anxiety in the face of existence have been stricken by sudden obsolescence. The language of theology lost its hold over the minds of even the most fervent believers. The language of philosophy is hardly possible. The language of science in its optimistic nineteenth century variety has suffered a loss of self-assurance. In this situation a poet trying to come to terms with experience has had to discover his or her own improvised means. That was not the case in the past, when poets worked with constant reference to images provided by religion and religiously oriented philosophy. Perhaps now poets are returning to the time of the pre-Socratics, to the unity of poetry and philosophy not yet conscious of their separate claims. In the poetry of the last decades there is a groping in that direction, a persistent effort to start from scratch in attempting to define our human condition. In Anna Swir's vision, we are alone in a world without gods, exposed to total annihilation every moment , helpless in the face of terminal illness and old age, driven to seek in each other's arms physical love as the only possible source of warmth and peace. Yet the exploration of the only tangible thing which is given us as ourself, namely our body, leads her to a paradoxical duality. Her personae are trapped by their flesh but also distinct from it, for they are consciousness, ever present, perhaps with rare exceptions – flashes of purely physical bliss. Her poetry is about not being identical with one's body, about sharing its joys and pains and still rebelling against its laws.

Anna is not an abstract figure for me. We made our literary debut more or less at the same time before the war, and later I used to see her, though not often, in underground Warsaw, where writers would attend clandestine meetings. When, after many years, I met her in Poland in the summer of 1981, she seemed to me much stronger – in the physical sense, too – than she had been in her youth: an attractive woman, lithe, with a ruddy complexion, her hair like the white mane of a fairy-tale witch. I told her that I had always valued her poetry, though at the moment I did not expect I would translate a volume of it into English.

Somehow the decision matured slowly and became a reality three years later, in 1984. Then, but not before the volume had been completed, I told her about my endeavors in a letter. From her an-

5

swer I could see that the news made her genuinely happy. I did not realize that she was at the time dangerously ill. A few weeks later I was stunned to hear she had died of cancer. Perhaps we all strongly believe in certain modes of behavior which should be effective means against death: an ecstatic approval of life, a clear awareness of our precarious human condition. To me Anna Swir seemed immune simply because it was difficult to imagine a person writing her type of poetry who was not strongly alive. What remained now was to think with relief that at least I brought some joy to the last days of her earthly peregrination.

That she did not write literary criticism is to her credit. Yet she was an artist well aware of what she was doing. In one of her infrequent pronouncements I find the following remarks on poetry:

"By expressing reality, poetry masters and overcomes it. Poetry creates around man a delicate, tender miniworld to protect him from the dreadfulness of the maxiworld. Every Negro or Eskimo lullaby is a warm nest for a human nestling, enveloping its helplessness. Let our words be as necessary and useful as once were words of magic. This is an unachievable ideal."

"The poet should be as sensitive as an aching tooth."

"[The poet] has a conscience with room to grow, what does not as yet shock and outrage others shocks and outrages him."

"How to write poems? There will be as many answers as people who write. Personally, I consider that nothing can replace the psychosomatic phenomenon of inspiration. This seems to me the only biologically natural way for a poem to be born and gives the poem something like a biological right to exist."

"The goal of words in poetry is to grow up to the contents, yet that goal cannot ever be attained, for only a small part of the psychic energy which dwells in a poet incarnates itself in words. In fact, every poem has the right to ask for a new poetics. This is created only once to express the contents, also given only once, of a poem.

Style is the enemy of a poet, and its greatest merit would be non-existence. We could say in paradoxical abbreviation that a writer has two tasks. The first – to create one's own style. The second – to destroy one's own style. The second is more difficult and takes more time."

Hers were quite severe demands and, I am sure, not to everybody's liking. Contrary to the widespread view that poetry is an act of spinning a linguistic thread, she advanced the idea of a transparent style aspiring to nonexistence because it strives to seize what she termed "contents." In this she proved loyal to her own development as a poet: moving from the highly stylized, detached miniatures of her youth to a form which is artless in appearance, and confesses that it is inadequate for the overbearing passions of a being, all flesh and blood.

I translated these poems and then showed them to my friend Leonard Nathan, whose poetic insight I trust. He read them carefully and marked all the places where the wording seemed doubtful to him, from the point of view of either American idiom or meaning. Then we sat down and worked together on the marked passages. As I value his contribution, I feel he should be considered a co-translator. We decided to open the volume with "Poems About My Father and My Mother" taken from her book published posthumously by her daughter, *Suffering and Joy*, 1985. At a time when this theme of "unhappy childhood" is fashionable, these poems are striking, as she appears in them again as a poet of love – for her parents.

In the Afterword we quote some of Anna Swir's war poems. There is a separate bilingual edition of her *Building the Barricade*, translated by Magnus J. Kryński and Robert A. Maguire, but published in 1979 in Kraków, Poland, and not available in this country except in some libraries.

– CZESŁAW MIŁOSZ

Poems About My Father and My Mother

A Cardboard Suitcase

My father was sixteen,
under his bed he kept a cardboard suitcase
with a hole in it.
In the suitcase there were a dirty shirt
and political tracts.

He passed these out where he was told to,
after quitting time.
His crew was then painting the ceiling in a theater.
He would leap
through scaffoldings, floors
down,
headlong.
He was sixteen.

My Father Would Recall

All his life my father
would recall the revolution
of Nineteen Five, how he carried
tracts with his comrades,
how he was on the Grzybow Square
when it all began, how the one
who stood to his right, pulled
from under his coat
a red banner and the one to his left
a revolver.

How he marched in a demonstration
in Marszalkowska Street and suddenly the charge
of Cossacks, above his head
horses' hooves, he was fleeing,
a Cossack cut off
his comrade's arm, it fell
on the pavement, another Cossack
cut off the head
of a woman, father was fleeing,
he had to flee
to America.

Father would sing till his death
songs from Nineteen Five.
Now
I sing them.

My Mother, Miss Stasia

When my mother walked in the Church Street
in the town of Ostroleka,
old Jewish women
would tsk tsk with admiration:
this is an angel.

She sang soprano
"Lute," in the singing society.
Handsome Mr. Raczynski
wanted to marry her. She broke
the engagement.

He despaired.
The Lord will punish you for me.
And the Lord punished her.
She married a madman.

Soup for the Poor

Through the streets of Warsaw
kitchens for the poor are hauled.
The poor stand in lines,
they warm themselves by bonfires
which are lit for them
in the streets of Warsaw.

It is the First World War.
Mother put on a kerchief,
covered her face, went out
into the street to stand in line
for the soup of the poor.

Mother was afraid
that the janitor's wife would see her.
Mother after all was
the wife of an artist.

An Artist Moves

At dawn
we leave on tiptoe.

Father carries the easel
and three paintings, mother
a chest and the eiderdown
inherited from grandmother, I myself
a pot and a teakettle.

We load it all on a cart, quickly,
so the janitor does not see.
My father
is pulling the cart, quickly,
my mother pushes at the rear, quickly,
I push also, quickly, quickly, quickly,
so that the janitor does not see.

We owe
a half-year's rent.

Before Dawn

You must line up
for twenty pounds of coal
before dawn.

Mother stands in icy cold, stomping,
the holes in her wet shoes stuffed
with paper.

Mother is glad
that I sleep in a warm bed.

White Wedding Slippers

At night
mother opened a chest and took out
her white wedding slippers
of silk. Then slowly
daubed them with ink.

Early in the morning
she went in those slippers
into the street
to line up for bread.
It was minus ten degrees,
she stood
for three hours in the street.

They were handing out
one-quarter of a loaf per person.

They Saved Me

Twenty-four hours
I was dying of fever.

Twenty-four hours
mother knelt
and prayed by my bed.

Twenty-four hours
father lay, face down
on the floor.

They saved me.

Three Pieces of Candy

I'm dizzy from hunger
and the child is pale as paper –
says mother to father
when we walk in the street.

– So buy each of us a bonbon
– says father.
– I have no money –
says mother.

And she buys each of us
a bonbon.
– Anyway, it gives you strength –
says mother.

We smile,
all three of us.
We taste. Three paradises melt
in our mouths.

I Am Eleven

I hate father's paintings.
All our misery is in them,
tears of my mother.
They suck our blood
like vampires, demand
a sacrifice of life, like gods.

I love father's paintings.
They are my brothers and sisters, my only
comrades, in the workshop
cut off like the struggle of a madman.

When nobody is home
I pass my ink-stained finger
through the flame
of the candle.
I want to become a saint,
I want to measure up to father's paintings.

I have no idea
that I hate, that I love,
that I want to measure up.

Vacations in Kurpieland

We wander all three of us
village to village, forest to forest
up to our ankles in hot sand.
Best is to walk barefoot.

Father collects from cottages
paper cut-outs, from garrets
he pulls out old paintings.

In the evening
I sleep over a clay tureen
of wild strawberries and milk,
over a hunk
of bread as dark as earth,
from a loaf that weighs
as much as I do.

My Father's Workshop

I owe my second birth
to my father's workshop.
Father painted its walls
black, it was sublime
like a coffin, on the black walls
tall stained-glass panels
hung, huge paintings
grew in corners, that was
power, they thronged,
every day taller, beating their wings
against the high ceiling, father
was painting in an overcoat, I was cold
and hungry, I used to sit
cross-legged on the floor,
we had no table, and I wrote
Latin verbs, in the alcove
the soup was boiling, mother,
sick, was lying there, I was
afraid she would die,
I would wake up at night
afraid they both would die,
I listened to their breathing, the window in the roof
was white with frost, the coal
used up, I thought
under my blanket that I
would be the Spirit-King, in the ceiling
there was a hook
from which a starving painter
who lived here
hanged himself.

Christmas Eve

A Christmas Eve for three of us.
Mother has washed the floors,
Father lights up the Christmas tree.
A wafer, a herring.

Mother is crying.
She sings the carol "Sleep well, sweet Jesus"
in the soprano of Miss Stasia,
a beauty
from the town of Ostroleka.

Beyond the window: night and frost and fear.
How good it is we're here,
we three.

He Did Not Jump from the Third Floor

The second World War.
Warsaw.
Tonight they dropped bombs
on the Theatre Square.

At the Theatre Square
Father has his workshop.
All paintings, labor
of forty years.

Next morning father went
to the Theatre Square.
He saw.

His workshop has no ceiling,
has no walls
no floor.

Father did not jump
from the third floor.
Father started over
from the beginning.

Father in Kraków

Eighty-year-old legs
carry him to the Wawel Castle.
He must verify each day
that the Wawel has not vanished over night.

After all, he has lived through a day
in which a house disappeared
with all his paintings
painted in hunger and cold
for forty years.

Mother Sings Again

For the first time in many years
I heard her singing
by the bed of her granddaughter.

She sang in the young soprano
of Miss Stasia, a beauty
from the town of Ostroleka.
Who married
a madman.

Mother Dying

When mother was going through agony of death
I had no time to cry
I had to help her
in her dying.

When it was over
I was a corpse myself.
Corpses do not cry.

She Came to Say Farewell

On the day after her death
mother came
to say farewell to me.

At night I heard
her steps nearing my bed
step
by step. She stopped
by my head.

I said: Mommy,
do not appear, Mommy,
my heart will burst
from fear.

No more than that
I said to her
by way of farewell.

In the Other World

In the other world
I will have lots of time.
I will be able to shed a thousand tears
for every tear she shed because of me.
I will be able to kiss the earth
at her feet. And knock my head against the earth.

– Forgive me.
And she will forgive.

Her Death is in Me

Only after mother's death,
I learned with amazement
that we were not
one person.

And it's precisely then,
more than any other time,
we became
one person.

Her living death
lived for long months
in my living flesh.
She was in me day and night,
I felt her
inside me, like a child.

Her death will be in me
till the end.

Calm Down

At night
the telephone rings.
I wake up, terrified.
– Something bad
happened to father.

Calm down – says my daughter.
Grandfather is just fine.
After all, he died
a month ago.

He Sang All His Life

Father
sang all his life.
When he was young, in Warsaw,
all winter, in the unheated workshop
he sang, his brush
gripped with fingers blue with cold.
When he came back and told mother
that he had not gotten a commission
for a portrait from a photograph,
and there was no bread for tomorrow,
he would take up his palette and start
to sing.

In Kraków when he had reached
Ninety
and, in a corner of his workshop,
high-ceilinged as a church

death was waiting behind a picture –
he would sing all morning
and evening.
He sang loudly and beautifully,
people would stop on the stairs,
listening
astonished.

When he died and his paintings
were removed from the workshop, I
started to sing.
– What are you doing – said my daughter.

Grandfather died and you sing
so loud you can hear it
on the stairs.

And I sang one after the other
all the songs he sang when he was young
and when he was ninety,
with death
waiting in a corner behind a picture
in a workshop as wretched
as any when he was young.

I sang for the last time
between high walls
black from soot,
where he had suffered for thirty years
and where he was taken
without pain
in his sleep
by death.
Who one night came silently out
from behind a painting in the corner.

Old Madman

For thirty years
he painted the same painting
nine feet wide,
The Entry of Queen Jadwiga to the Wawel Castle.
He would scrape away the paint
every few days
and begin again.
Whole days and nights
till sunrise.

After his death
the painting cracks, rigid with dried oil.
It probably will die without achieving
fame.
As he did not achieve it,
old madman
who for thirty years
till sunrise
would paint and then destroy what he'd done.

I Wash the Shirt

For the last time I wash the shirt
of my father who died.
The shirt smells of sweat. I remember
that sweat from my childhood,
so many years
I washed his shirts and underwear,
I dried them
at an iron stove in the workshop,
he would put them on unironed.

From among all the bodies in the world,
animal, human,
only one exuded that sweat.
I breathe it in
for the last time. Washing this shirt
I destroy it
forever.
Now
only paintings survive him
which smell of oils.

He Strode Against the Tide

He walked the streets of Kraków,
an old crank who had failed,

He painted like no one else,
lived like no one else,
painted huge canvases,
was rude like Socrates.
The list of Polish painters
did not include his name.

All his life he strode
against the tide.

A Film About My Father

They show a film about my father,
in that film
father is quiet, it's I
who shout against his tragedy,
stutter, comically
gesticulate.

In the audience
are the art connoisseurs. Why
is that woman so worked up?
After all we know
who is truly great.
We drink vodka with the truly great.
Whoever heard of him?
She compares him to Norwid,
crazy female.

We Survived Them

For a solemn opening
of his post-mortem exhibit
he will arrive and stand by me
in his old grey sweater.
Stooping,
strong.

Nobody will see him
only I will look at him.
He will say:
– We survived them.

Wind

I Am Filled with Love

I am filled with love
as a great tree with the wind,
as a sponge with the ocean,
as a great life with suffering,
as time with death.

Happiness

My hair is happy
and my skin is happy.
My skin quivers with happiness.

I breathe happiness instead of air,
slowly and deeply,
as a man who avoided a mortal danger.

Tears roll down my face,
I do not know it.
I forget I still have a face.
My skin is singing,
I shiver.

I feel time's duration
as it felt in the hour of death.
As if my sense of time alone were grasping the world,
as if existence were time only.
Immersed in terrifying
magnificence
I feel every second of happiness, as it arrives,
fills up, bursts into flower
according to its own natural way,
unhurried as a fruit,
astounding as a deity.

Now
I begin to scream.
I am screaming. I leave my body.
I do not know whether I am human anymore,

how could anyone know that, screaming with happiness.
Yet one dies from such screaming,
thus I am dying from happiness.
On my face there are probably no more tears,
my skin probably does not sing by now.
I don't know whether I still have a skin,
from me to my skin
is too far to know.

Soon I will go.
I do not shiver any longer,
I do not breathe any longer.
I don't know whether I still have
something to breathe with.

I feel time's duration,
how perfectly I feel time's duration.

I sink
I sink into time.

Woman Unborn

I am not born as yet,
five minutes before my birth.
I can still go back
into my unbirth.
Now it's ten minutes before,
now, it's one hour before birth.
I go back,
I run
into my minus life.

I walk through my unbirth as in a tunnel
with bizarre perspectives.
Ten years before,
a hundred and fifty years before,
I walk, my steps thump,
a fantastic journey through epochs
in which there was no me.

How long is my minus life,
nonexistence so much resembles immortality.

Here is Romanticism, where I could have been a spinster,
Here is the Renaissance, where I would have been
an ugly and unloved wife of an evil husband,
The Middle Ages, where I would have carried water
    in a tavern.

I walk still farther,
what an echo,
my steps thump

through my minus life,
through the reverse of life.
I reach Adam and Eve,
nothing is seen anymore, it's dark.
Now my nonexistence dies already
with the trite death of mathematical fiction.
As trite as the death of my existence would have been
had I been really born.

Troubles with the Soul at Morning Calisthenics

Lying down I lift my legs,
my soul by mistake jumps into my legs.
This is not convenient for her,
besides, she must branch,
for the legs are two.

When I stand on my head
my soul sinks down to my head.
She is then in her place.

But how long can you stand on your head,
especially if you do not know
how to stand on your head.

Myself and My Person

There are moments
when I feel more clearly than ever
that I am in the company
of my own person.
This comforts and reassures me,
this heartens me,
just as my tridimensional body
is heartened by my own authentic shadow.

There are moments
when I really feel more clearly than ever
that I am in the company
of my own person.

I stop
at a street corner to turn left
and I wonder what would happen
if my own person walked to the right.

Until now that has not happened
but it does not settle the question.

Maternity

I gave birth to life.
It went out of my entrails
and asks for the sacrifice of my life
as does an Aztec deity.
I lean over a little puppet,
we look at each other
with four eyes.

"You are not going to defeat me," I say
"I won't be an egg which you would crack
in a hurry for the world,
a footbridge that you would take on the way to your life.
I will defend myself."

I lean over a little puppet,
I notice
a tiny movement of a tiny finger
which a little while ago was still in me,
in which, under a thin skin,
my own blood flows.
And suddenly I am flooded
by a high, luminous wave
of humility.
Powerless, I drown.

A Visit

In a home for incurables
I visited a woman who was about to die.
She embraced me,
I felt through her gray shirt
the tiny bones of her brittle body
which would no longer arouse lust or tenderness.

"I don't want this, take me away."
Near us, a retarded woman was vomiting.

Seventy Years

He never wanted to enter my place.
"I stink, Mrs. S., it's my feet,
They're rotting,
every day I spread ashes on them,
ash has a mystical meaning,
I brought you some apples from my garden."

Once he wrote me a letter, that he would poison himself
with rat poison.
I arrived too late,
his wife was crying.
"He studied yoga, Mrs. S.
A retired stationmaster.
He collected old cans, newspapers, bolts,
his room full, read mystics.
At night he would stand in the garden
in his drawers.
Hands raised,
he waited for the revelation of the truth
for seventy years.
Obviously he could not wait longer."

Their women neighbors said to me:
"It's fortunate for her that he died.
She had to spread ashes every day on them.
Pus, you understand,
It stank bad, he hollered at her."

Tears

The old woman cries,
she coddles herself in her crying
as a bird in its nest.
She sinks
into the depth of crying.
She immerses herself
in dark immersion.
Tears run down her face
like little warm animals.
They stroke her old face,
they take pity on her.

The last rapture
of tears.

Terminally Ill

Every morning he is astounded again,
always for the first time,
every time more violently than before.

He is astounded relentlessly,
with impressive energy,
passionately, fiercely, vehemently,
till he is out of breath.

He pants with astonishment,
he chokes,
he gluts himself on astonishment,
he drowns like a puppy thrown into deep water,
he shivers, trembles, cries with astonishment.

That the affliction came to him
against which there is no help.

My Suffering

My suffering
is useful to me.

It gives me the privilege
to write on the suffering of others.

My suffering is a pencil
with which I write.

To Be a Woman

A Woman Talks to Her Thigh

It is only thanks to your good looks
I can take part
in the rites of love.

Mystical ecstasies,
treasons delightful
as a crimson lipstick,
a perverse rococo
of psychological involutions,
sweetness of carnal longings
that take your breath,
pits of despair
sinking to the very bottom of the world:
all this I owe to you.

How tenderly every day I should
lash you with a whip of cold water,
if you alone allow me to possess
beauty and wisdom
irreplaceable.

The souls of my lovers
open to me in a moment of love
and I have them in my dominion.
I look as does a sculptor
on his work
at their faces snapped shut with eyelids,
martyred by ecstasy,
made dense by happiness.
I read as does an angel

thoughts in their skulls,
I feel in my hand
a beating human heart,
I listen to the words
which are whispered by one human to another
in the frankest moments of one's life.

I enter their souls,
I wander
by a road of delight or of horror
to lands as inconceivable
as the bottoms of the oceans.
Later on, heavy with treasures
I come slowly
to myself.

O, many riches,
many precious truths
growing immense in a metaphysical echo,
many initiations
delicate and startling
I owe to you, my thigh.

The most exquisite refinement of my soul
would not give me any of those treasures
if not for the clear, smooth charm
of an amoral little animal.

FELICIA'S LOVE:

Three Bodies

A pregnant woman
lies at night by her man.
In her belly
a child moved.
"Put your hand on my belly,"
says the woman.
"What moved so lightly
is a tiny hand or leg
of our child.
It will be mine and yours
though only I have to bear it,"

The man nestles close to her,
they both feel the same.
In the woman a child moves.

And the three bodies pool their warmth
at night, when a pregnant woman
lies by her man.

You Are Warm

You are warm
like a big dog. I bask
in your warmth. I immerse myself
in purity.

Every day I put on my neck
the corals of your young enchantment.
I plait into my hair your tenderness.
Your calm
strokes me on the head.

You have the virgin charm
of a being who has never experienced
the kiss of pain or the embrace of fear.

Leaning over you
I look into your eyes.
Undisturbed by thought, they reflect
the sky.

I Sleep in Blue Pajamas

I sleep in blue pajamas,
at my right my child sleeps.
I have never cried,
I will never die.

I sleep in blue pajamas,
at my left my man sleeps.
I have never knocked my head against the wall,
I have never screamed out of fear.

How large this bed is
if it had room enough
for such happiness.

What is a Pineal Gland

You lie asleep,
warm as a small heating plant.
Your lungs move, viscera digest,
glands diligently work,
biological processes of your sleep
make grow
the vegetation of dreams.

Do you belong to me?
I myself do not belong to you.

I touch my skin,
lungs move inside me,
viscera digest,
the body performs its work
with which I am not acquainted.
I know so little about the activity of the pineal gland.
Really, what do I have in common
with my body.

I touch your skin and my skin,
I am not in you
and you are not in me.
It's cold here.
Homeless, I tremble looking
at our two bodies
warm and quiet.

You Sleep

Falling asleep
you ask me whether I am happy.

Over our bed, death
stands and looks at me
through your body as if through glass
with the marbles of his lidless eyes.

Under our bed
a precipice up to the stars.
Shelter my eyes with your hands
o my warm man,
shelter my eyes with your living hands.

You sleep already.

Male and Female

You inseminated me and I gave birth to pearls.
Authentic pearls. Look.

You look, amazed,
that wealth terrifies you,
you don't understand it.

You, pebble who moved an avalanche,
look how resplendent
is its panting glamour.
Listen to a heavy hymn
of falling.

You, a pebble without eyes and ears.

Tears Stream

They are dying, clasped tenderly to one another,
bound by their suffering
as once they were by love.
Unable to live together,
necessary to each other at that moment of dying,
close to each other
in that moment only.

Their embrace is ice,
they depart together fulfilling their oath
that they would not forsake each other till death.

Her tears
roll down his naked arm,
his tears stream
between her naked breasts.

Then
they both harden
like a sculpture on an Etruscan sarcophagus.

My Body Effervesces

I am born for the second time.
I am light
as the eyelash of the wind.
I froth, I am froth.

I walk dancing,
if I wish, I will soar.
The condensed lightness
of my body
condenses most forcibly
in the lightness of my foot
and its five toes.
The foot skims the earth
which gives way like compressed air.
An elastic duo
of the earth and of the foot. A dance
of liberation.

I am born for the second time,
happiness of the world
came to me again.
My body effervesces,
I think with my body which effervesces.

If I wish
I will soar.

ANTONIA'S LOVE:

A Bitch

You come to me at night,
you are an animal.
A woman and an animal can be joined
by the night only.
Maybe you are a wild he-goat,
or perhaps a rabid dog.
Hard to tell in the dark.

I say tender words to you,
you don't understand, you are an animal.
You are not surprised
that sometimes I cry.

But your animal body
understands more than you do.
It, too, is sad.
And when you fall asleep
it warms me up with its hairy warmth.
We sleep hugging each other
like two puppies who lost their bitch.

A Spring

The greatest happiness you give me
is that I don't love you.
Freedom.

I bask by you
in the warmth of that freedom,
I am meek
with the meekness of strength
and sensitive,
alert as spring.

In all my hugs
there is a readiness to leave.
As in the body of an athlete
a future leap.

I Cannot

I envy you. Every moment
You can leave me.

I cannot
leave myself.

[ANTONIA'S LOVE]

Iron Currycomb

Don't come to me today.
Had I half-opened the door
you wouldn't have recognized my face.
For I am busy with stocktaking,
with capital repair, balance of accounts.
This is my washing day,
a dress rehearsal for the end of the world
in microcosm.

With an iron currycomb
I scrub my body to the bone,
I have taken the skin off the bones,
it is hanging over there,
naked intestines smoke,
naked ribs quiver
and the trial goes on,
the most high court of justice
is going to proceed in a summary manner.
All verdicts will be sentences.

It judges the brain and the eyes taken out of the skull,
the sinful nakedness of the pelvis
and of the teeth without gums,
unclean lungs, lazy tibia.
Oh, I toil hard,
with an iron currycomb
I scrub my body to the bone,

70

the bone to the marrow.
I want to be cleaner than the bone.
I want to be clean
as nothingness.

I judge, I carry out sentences,
I shiver with terror,
both the condemned one and the tired executioner,
I balance accounts, I sweat
with bloody sweat.

So don't come to me today.
Don't buy flowers, it's a waste of money.

[ANTONIA'S LOVE]

Go to a Western

I enjoy equally
my greeting you and my saying good-bye.
Thus you give me
two pleasures.

But today don't come.
I have guests. A visit of
Weariness with Love's Ritual,
A Mocking Glance of Eternity and
Disgust.

They are strangers, you don't know their languages.
So better go to a Western.

The Same Inside

Walking to your place for a love feast
I saw on a street corner
an old beggar woman.

I took her hand,
kissed her delicate cheek,
we talked, she was
the same inside as I am,
from the same kind,
I sensed this instantly
as a dog knows by scent
another dog.

I gave her money,
I could not part from her.
After all, one needs
someone who is close.

And then I no longer knew
why I was walking to your place.

Large Intestine

Look in the mirror. Let us both look.
Here is my naked body.
Apparently you like it,
I have no reason to.
Who bound us, me and my body?
Why must I die
together with it?
I have the right to know where the borderline
between us is drawn.
Where am I, I, I myself?

Belly, am I in the belly? In the intestines?
In the hollow of the sex? In a toe?
Apparently in the brain. I do not see it.
Take my brain out of my skull. I have the right
to see myself. Don't laugh.
That's macabre, you say.

It's not me who made
my body.
I wear the used rags of my family,
an alien brain, fruit of chance, hair
after my grandmother, the nose
glued together from a few dead noses.
What do I have in common with all that?
What do I have in common with you, who like
my knee, what is my knee to me?

74

Surely
I would have chosen a different model.

I will leave both of you here,
my knee and you.
Don't make a wry face, I will leave you all my body
to play with.
And I will go.
There is no place for me here,
in this blind darkness waiting for
corruption.
I will run out, I will race
away from myself.
I will look for myself
running
like crazy
till my last breath.

One must hurry
before death comes. For by then
like a dog jerked by its chain
I will have to return
into this stridently suffering body.
To go through the last
most strident ceremony of the body.

Defeated by the body,
slowly annihilated because of the body
I will become kidney failure
or the gangrene of the large intestine.
And I will expire in shame.

And the universe will expire with me,
reduced as it is
to a kidney failure
and the gangrene of the large intestine.

[ANTONIA'S LOVE]

I'll Open the Window

Our embrace lasted too long.
We loved right down to the bone.
I hear the bones grind, I see
our two skeletons.

Now I am waiting
till you leave, till
the clatter of your shoes
is heard no more. Now, silence.

Tonight I am going to sleep alone
on the bedclothes of purity.
Aloneness
is the first hygienic measure.
Aloneness
will enlarge the walls of the room,
I will open the window
and the large, frosty air will enter,
healthy as tragedy.
Human thoughts will enter
and human concerns,
misfortune of others, saintliness of others.
They will converse softly and sternly.

Do not come anymore.
I am an animal
very rarely.

In Railway Stations

There, crazy hags
who carry all their belongings
in a bundle on their back.

Homeless who huddle
at night in railway stations.
Patients who wait in a hospital
for the last operation.

And I lost so much time
with you.

Nonexistent

Where are you, friend,
pure as plant life,
more faithful
than my own body.
The earth gives birth to millions of people
but you are not born.

There is not even a silence
waiting for your voice,
no space
waiting for the shadow
of your moving hand.

Nonexistent,
come to me.

STEPHANIE'S LOVE:

A Gentle World

We are joined together by the heaven
of Fra Angelico.
His childish angels
give us their fingers.

His smile we will take in our knapsack
wandering together
through a spring world
which is gentle as the death of a blessed man.

[STEPHANIE'S LOVE]

The Youngest Children of an Angel

When you kissed me for the first time
we became a couple
of the youngest children of an angel,
which just started
to fledge.

Lapsed into a silence in mid-move,
hushed in mid-breath,
astounded
to the very blood,
they listen with their bodies
to the sprouting on their shoulder blades
of the first little plume.

In a Crimson Gondola

I don't love you, but the happiness
which I give you.

It joins us
as a crimson gondola
joins a young doge and his bride
the day of their wedding.

The First Madrigal

That night of love was pure
as an antique musical instrument
and the air around it.

Rich
as a ceremony of coronation.
It was fleshy as a belly of a woman in labor
and spiritual
as a number.

It was only a moment of life
and it wanted to be a conclusion drawn from life.
By dying
it wanted to comprehend the principle of the world.

That night of love
had ambitions.

The Second Madrigal

A night of love
exquisite as a
concert from old Venice
played on exquisite instruments.
Healthy as a
buttock of a little angel.
Wise as an
anthill.
Garish as air
blown into a trumpet.
Abundant as the reign
of a royal Negro couple
seated on two thrones
cast in gold.

A night of love with you,
a big baroque battle
and two victories.

An Iron Hedgehog

A happy woman,
I am as an embryo in the mother's womb,
I sleep hidden in you.

Don't give birth to me yet,
I want to be in you always.
Here is my warmth,
my refuge.

Now I don't exist at all outside of you,
I am nowhere else
and that is good.

The world is freezing, I am afraid,
it is like a hedgehog with quills of iron and ice.
Do not ever give birth to me.
I want to sleep in you.

A Plate of Suffering

This morning
a vast new world
is created for me,
especially for me, what a luxury!
The world of suffering.

Outside the window a city
of the world of suffering.
Here is an authentic
street of that city.
Here is a table, a plate, a spoon.
A spoon solidly suffering, a true
plate of suffering. I will eat my breakfast
on it today.

Before my house a car and a driver
both spick-and-span,
just as if real, but this is an appearance.
Yesterday they did not exist.
They were made today
especially for me. What a luxury.

No effort was spared. Even a fly
which sits at the edge of a piece of paper
while I write, is a new one,
a fly of the world of suffering.

That world was offered to me
so suddenly. It is a precious and rare gift
like a noose of diamonds.

I wonder at it. My hands
grow cold out of wonder.
Convex eyelids
close softly
on my eyes.

[STEPHANIE'S LOVE]

Virginity

One must be brave to live through
a day. What remains
is nothing but the pleasure of longing – very precious.

Longing
purifies as does flying, strengthens as does an effort,
it fashions the soul
as work
fashions the belly.

It is like an athlete, like a runner
who will never
stop running. And this
gives him endurance.

Longing
is nourishing for the strong.
It is like a window
on a high tower, through which
blows the wind of strength.

Longing,
Virginity of happiness.

Other Poems

Happy as a Dog's Tail

Happy as something unimportant
and free as a thing unimportant.
As something no one prizes
and which does not prize itself.
As something mocked by all
and which mocks at their mockery.
As laughter without serious reason.
As a yell able to outyell itself.
Happy as no matter what, as any no matter what.

Happy
as a dog's tail.

I Starve My Belly for a Sublime Purpose

Three days
I starve my belly
so that it learns
to eat the sun.

I say to it: Belly,
I am ashamed of you. You must
spiritualize yourself. You must
eat the sun.

The belly keeps silent
for three days. It's not easy
to waken in it higher aspirations.

Yet I hope for the best.
This morning, tanning myself on the beach,
I noticed that, little by little,
it begins to shine.

I Knocked My Head Against the Wall

As a child
I put my finger in the fire
to become
a saint.

As a teenager
every day I would knock my head against the wall.

As a young girl
I went out through a window of a garret
to the roof
in order to jump.

As a woman
I had lice all over my body.
They cracked when I was ironing my sweater.

I waited sixty minutes
to be executed.
I was hungry for six years.

Then I bore a child,
they were carving me
without putting me to sleep.

Then a thunderbolt killed me
three times and I had to rise from the dead three times
without anyone's help.

Now I am resting
after three resurrections.

I Say to My Body: You Carcass

TO ARTUR SANDAUER

I say to my body
– You carcass – I say,
You carcass, crated, nailed down,
deaf and blind
like a padlock.

I should beat you till you scream,
Starve you for forty days,
hang you over the highest abyss of the world.

Perhaps then a window in you would open
on everything I feel exists,
on everything that is closed to me.

I say to my body:
you carcass,
you are afraid of pain and hunger,
you are afraid
of the abyss.
You, deaf, blind carcass – I say
and I spit at the mirror.

I Sleep and Snore

My legs snore,
my hands snore,
my belly snores
like insolence.
I am the capital of the empire of snoring.

The complete happiness,
so to speak.

I Protest

Dying
is the hardest
work of all.

The old and sick
should be exempt from it.

Thing Indescribable

Out of suffering, power is born.
Out of power, suffering is born.

Two words for one
indescribable
thing.

She Does Not Remember

She was an evil stepmother.
In her old age she is slowly dying
in an empty hovel.

She shudders
like a wad of burning paper.
She does not remember that she was evil.
But she knows
that she feels cold.

The Greatest Love

She is sixty. She lives
the greatest love of her life.

She walks arm-in-arm with her dear one,
her hair streams in the wind.
Her dear one says:
"You have hair like pearls."

Her children say:
"Old fool."

The Old Woman

Her beauty
is like Atlantis.
It is yet to be discovered.
Thousands of humorists
have written about her erotic desires.
The most gifted of them
entered the school reading lists.
Only her making love with the devil
had the seriousness
of fire around the stake
and was within the human imagination just as was
    the fire.

Mankind created for her
the most abusive
words of the world.

A Conversation with a Little Flower

Don't die, little flower.
I'll die instead.

You're so innocent and clean,
so infinitely more
deserving of immortality.

The Sea and Man

You will not tame this sea
either by humility or rapture.
But you can laugh
in its face.

Laughter
was invented by those
who live briefly
as a burst of laughter.

The eternal sea
will never learn to laugh.

To That Which is Most Important

Were I able to shut
my eyes, ears, legs, hands
and walk into myself
for a thousand years,
perhaps I would reach
– I do not know its name –
what matters most.

Poetry Reading

I'm curled into a ball
like a dog
that is cold.

Who will tell me
why I was born,
why this monstrosity
called life.

The telephone rings. I have to give
a poetry reading.

I enter.
A hundred people, a hundred pairs of eyes.
They look, they wait.
I know for what.

I am supposed to tell them
why they were born,
why there is
this monstrosity called life.

I Must Fight an Angel

I must fight an angel
inherited
from my father and my mother.

He fed on their tears, ate the grass
of their misfortunes,
drank from the pure source
of their suffering.
He grew up handsome and angelic,
his skin
invisible – no, he
has no skin.
He devours my skin, my fur,
my claws, my teeth,
my defenses against the world.

Perhaps I will kill my angel.
Perhaps he will kill me.

I Do Not Accept

I renounce this fingernail
already worn
by my grandfather.
This head occupied
for two thousand years
by the bloody body of Julius Caesar.

The dead sit on me
like a mountain. The carrion
of barbaric epochs,
of bodies and thoughts decays in me.
Cruel corpses of centuries
ask
that I be as cruel as they.

But I am not going to repeat
their dead words.
I have to give myself
a new birth. I have to
give birth to a new time.

Goddess of Matriarchy

Your bones are made of wealth, your meat of happiness,
your veins, of gold.
Your body is a golden house of Solomon,
it is an Eiffel tower, your hands
support the weight of the sky with ten fingers
which are like ten superhuman fiery carrots,
ten lightning rods
hard as the Gothic.

Rigid with strength
like a coronation shirt
of Vishnu and Shiva,
like the eternal ice continent of Antarctica,
you will arrive
for the future must arrive.

You will arrive on your legs thick as power,
you, powerful
as a million years of fire
enclosed in a million years of ice.
And you will open your mouth
walled shut for a million years.

And you will bring to the world
stone tablets
of a new decalogue
not stained with blood.

That Would Not Be Good

When I am alone
I am afraid to turn
too quickly.

What is behind my back
may not, after all, be ready
to take a shape suitable
for human eyes.

And that would not be good.

Priceless Gifts

An empty day without events.
And that is why
it grew immense
as space. And suddenly
happiness of being
entered me.

I heard
in my heartbeat
the birth of time
and each instant of life
one after the other
came rushing in
like priceless gifts.

Like an Egyptian

I want to be so pure
that my body
will cast no shadow.
So that like a dead Egyptian
inside I will have no entrails.

So that in place of entrails
I will have light.

Four Very Fat Legs

I am jolly as if I were
very fat.
As if I had four
very fat legs. As if I jumped very high
on my four very fat legs.
As if I barked
cheerfully and very loudly
with those four very fat legs.
That's how jolly I am today.

Falling Asleep

I yawn,
I stretch,
I stretch out,
I stretch all over
in my body
as in a large, luxurious sleeping bag.

And then I fall
down,
down
to the bottom of happiness.

The Soul and the Body on the Beach

The soul on the beach
studies a textbook of philosophy.
The soul asks the body:
Who bound us together?
The body says:
Time to tan the knees.

The soul asks the body:
Is it true
that we do not really exist?
The body says:
I'm tanning my knees.

The soul asks the body:
Where will the dying begin,
in you or in me?
The body laughs,
It tanned its knees.

A Handy Sun

I like to warm myself
by the sun inside me.
Slowly I stretch
my four paws and my tail,
I close my eyes
and purr.

How good to own
a portable sun.

There is a Light in Me

Whether in daytime or in nighttime
I always carry inside
a light.
In the middle of noise and turmoil
I carry silence.
Always
I carry light and silence.

I Am Running on the Beach

I am running on the beach.
People puzzled.
– A grey-haired hag and she runs.

I am running on the beach
with an insolent look.
People laugh.
– Grey-haired and insolent.
They like that.

I Do Not Know How to Bark

I am washing the kitchen floor
on all four paws,
in the position of a dog.
I achieve
for a while
the good humor
of a dog.

Too bad, I just can't
bark.

I Am Raking Hay

I am raking hay
hurry, hurry
rain is coming.

In a cloud of hay
I run, I leap.
There is hay under my shirt,
fragrant hay.

We must build
four stacks
hurry hurry
rain is coming.

If there is manual labor in paradise
I request
work harvesting hay.

When I Am Digging Potatoes

I am digging potatoes for dinner,
an ant climbs my naked leg.
– Ant, what do you think
of eternity?

The ant has a superhuman face
like chemical processes
in the sun.
The ant can educate me
in questions of eternity.

Digging potatoes
improves the mind.

A Woman Writer Does Laundry

Enough typing.
Today I am doing laundry
in the old style.
I wash, I wash, rinse, wring
as did my grandmothers and great-grandmothers.
Relaxation.

Doing laundry is healthful and useful
like a washed shirt. Writing
is suspect.
Like three interrogation marks
typed on a page.

I Talk to My Body

My body, you are an animal
whose appropriate behavior
is concentration and discipline.
An effort
of an athlete, of a saint and of a yogi.

Well trained
you may become for me
a gate
through which I will leave myself
and a gate
through which I will enter myself.
A plumb line to the center of the earth
and a cosmic ship to Jupiter.

My body, you are an animal
for whom ambition
is right.
Splendid possibilities
are open to us.

By the Well

You, violent as a straight line
let me make you drink
from a bubbling well of irony.

A Dirty Sexy Poem

In order to heat up
their icy metaphysical pith
they submerge together
in hot excrement.

Sad Lovers

Like an eye and an eyelid
United by a tear.

It is Not Easy

I put on handcuffs
and leg irons
and now
I sprint.

A Double Rapture

Because there is no me
and because I feel
how much there is no me.

Poems About My Friend

Love with Rucksacks

Two rucksacks,
two grey heads.
And the roads of all the world
for wandering.

Our Two Silences

Silence
flows into me and out of me
washing my past away.
I am pure already, waiting for you. Bring me
your silence.

They will doze off
nested in each other's arms,
our two silences.

Beach Sandals

I swam away from myself.
Do not call me.
Swim away from yourself, too.

We will swim away, leaving our bodies
on the shore
like a pair of beach sandals.

Like a He-Bear and a She-Bear

Our feet are drunk
on our wide wandering
like bears with honey.
They walk slower and slower, humming
satiation.

Let us sit under a tree, my dear,
we will fall asleep together
like a he-bear by a she-bear.

Tell Me

Tell me, my dearest
now when I listen
to your heart beating,
when I drink from a little spring of warmth
in your neck,
when I look into you
as if you were transparent,
and see every thought of yours
and know
that you would die for me
were it necessary,
tell me now
whether we are the happiest
of all people
or the most unhappy.

Anxiety

You make among the trees
a nest for our love.
But look at the flowers
you've crushed.

Thank You, My Fate

Great humility fills me,
great purity fills me,
I made love with my dear
as if I made love dying
as if I made love praying,
tears pour
over my arms and his arms.
I don't know whether this is joy
or grief, I don't understand
what I feel, I'm crying,
I'm crying, it's humility
as if I were already dead,
gratitude, I thank you, my fate,
I am unworthy, how beautiful
my life.

I Look with My Eyes Flooded by Tears

I gave him pain
though I wanted so much
to give him happiness.

And he took it
delicately, as one takes
happiness. In daytime
he keeps it over his heart,
sleeps with it at night,
loves it as he loves me.
More than I do
it deserves love,
it is more pure and faithful.

I see how he bears it,
his shoulders
are more and more bent
under its weight.
I see with my eyes flooded by tears.

How he bears the pain I gave him,
though I wanted so much
to give him happiness.

Take My Pain

I said:
– Take my pain,
I am afraid of it,
it gnaws at
my warm entrails.
I want to live,
I am afraid of it,
take my pain, carry it for me.

He said:
– I will take your pain,
I will carry
both mine and yours.

He took it
and carries both. Lower and lower
he bends under its weight.

My Friend Speaks When Dying

It's getting close
the moment of leaving.
My heart is like a candlestick
with a hundred arms, lighted
for the ritual of dying.

In my heart a tall flame
of feeling glitters,
a flame of regret and a flame of fear
and also a flame
of love.

I say farewell to the earthly stars,
to the earthly sun, to trees
in the forests and to the wind on the roads,
I say farewell to Anna.

I bless people
I have known and people unknown
to me. Those who did me good
and those who did me evil.

And these words I pronounce are as important
as the words of a king.
I am like a king at this moment
when my being fades
so that I begin to be.

While I suffer
in a hospital bed in Warsaw.

Afterword: A Dialogue (1985)

NATHAN: The voice of these poems is that of a woman seemingly isolated from or indifferent to moral and social concerns. Anna Swir's voice comes out of a place with no local reality, a time with no differentiation except for moments of intensity. How does one position her in Polish poetic tradition? What would the Polish reader bring to the poems to make them seem less agonizingly pure intensity? Or is this original with her?

MIŁOSZ: There has been a tendency in Polish poetry of the last decades to search for expression in as few words as possible. That's part, I should say, of a certain trend connected with the abandonment of meters and rhymes, which occurred in good measure before the Second World War. In Swir's case, there is a conscious attempt to practice the art of the miniature, to create a situation within a few movements of the pen. One is reminded of drawings where everything is reduced to the bodies of two lovers, and the background is hardly indicated. There is a double movement: this tendency in postwar Polish poetry, and also her personal search for concision, which was already noticeable in her prewar poems.

NATHAN: In one of the poems we didn't use for this anthology, a woman talks about her life. She writes:

> Wind drives me on the roads,
> wind, a deity of change,
> with puffing cheeks.
> I love that wind,
> I rejoice
> in changes.

The poem goes on to praise her solitary walks. Whether we see the wind as some élan vital or as the passions that drive her, there's no beginning, there's no end; all we have is what she calls "longing and the death of longing / which is called fulfillment." This is a desolate vision. More than a matter of reducing technique to some minimum, her poetry seems the expression of a strong attitude toward the nature of things. What, beyond technical interest or striving, is in this kind of poem?

MIŁOSZ: Perhaps, Leonard, we talk of her slightly differently now because we have received word that she has died. But quite independently of that, Swir's poetry is poignant and pathetic; she exemplifies the situation of a modern woman, to a large extent. This is an emancipated woman, who is, in fact, rather lonely. In the poem you quoted, she appears as moving forward, marching with the wind, drawn by the wind or pushed by that wind, and she meets companions, but basically she is alone. I feel that she presents one aspect, maybe a dim aspect, maybe a less joyous aspect, of a woman's life in the twentieth century.

NATHAN: That I can see; the poems could be taken as feminist poems. Swir has a companion, Czesław, and that's her body. The mind and the body are split, and she frequently addresses her body as if it were an animal or a stranger she happens to know well; its address to her is pain and pleasure. Often there's no way of bringing them together. You get the impression she's a materialist, but how can a materialist be a dualist? And what a lonely dualism! Her isolation is even greater than just not having a companion for very long on the road; she's not even completely with her own body.

MIŁOSZ: That's a very good point that you have formulated very well: she has a companion, her body. Of course, Swir's philosophy is purely materialistic. She is outside any religion, any religious belief; she has only her body. But what I kept thinking as I read and translated her poems is that the duality of the soul and body is so persistent, something probably more fundamental than any religious belief. She reaches that gut feeling we have that we are not completely either the soul or the body. The body interferes with our soul; the soul interferes with our body.

NATHAN: And the marriage of the two is not a happy one. In the medieval debate between body and soul, the soul always gets the upper hand because it can look to a reward in heaven. One of the painful things about the debate here is that the body doesn't win, but the soul doesn't win either; they both meet the same fate.

MIŁOSZ: Here the soul (and be cautious now), consciousness, is confronted with the body. The body is the source of pleasure, of ecstasy – of sexual ecstasy, first of all. At the same time it is an enormous burden: the body goes toward death and drags the soul together with it. Consciousness kicks against it, doesn't want to go, but is dragged by the body; and this is the whole tragedy. If we look from that point of view, we see a very dramatic touch in these passionate poems.

NATHAN: Would that explain the anger and scorn that Swir sometimes has for her lovers? Is the real anger over the mortality of human relationships, which are the only ones that the body or the mind can look forward to – temporary relationships, transient, full of pain? Is the anger that of the mind in relation to all bodies, including those of her lovers?

MIŁOSZ: I guess so, because the encounter is on the level of the flesh, and there are several poems where any deeper relationship is questioned.

I would define Swir's poetry as somatic poetry. That's why I was interested in it. It is somatic poetry, but it becomes metaphysical, so to say, against her will: by faithfully describing soma, the flesh, she comes to a duality and to a nearly Platonic distance from the flesh. It's a tremendous paradox, but she, I believe, is lucid, very brutal and lucid; you can see that.

NATHAN: This raises another question about the technique of the poems. They're very terse; there's no involved syntax, no complicated diction. There's not much interest in psychology, certainly not that of the other person; she does a very quick job of psychology in the erotic situation, but not much more. I was wondering whether reducing the form that she uses is a reflection of this attempt to stay outside of complicated relationships, which to her are not true or lasting, but are illusions.

MIŁOSZ: It seems to me that here is the difference between her poetry and the poetry of American woman poets. They are deep into psychology. She is an anti-psychological poet in the sense that she deals with the situation of a man and a woman, but hardly in any particularized relationship. Of course she cannot eliminate human psychology completely, but it is looked at from a distance; she looks at herself, and her lover, coldly from a distance. There are varieties of relationships – for instance, in her poems there are three personae: Antonia, Stephanie, and Felicia. The relationships of those three women to men are different, but only, I should say, as three archetypes are different.

NATHAN: One thing missing from the register of possibilities is a relationship which is warm, ongoing, sympathetic. The relationhip at some point or other becomes antagonism, or an opposition, or a contrary. If a poem starts out to be romantic or sentimental, it doesn't end that way.

MIŁOSZ: There is no "and they lived happily ever after."

NATHAN: How did World War II and the war poems change Anna Swir as a poet?

MIŁOSZ: Swir entered the war as a very gifted and sophisticated young poet who wrote miniatures based mostly upon her experience of painting and medieval poetry. In 1942 in Nazi-occupied Warsaw I published her long poem entitled "The Year of 1941," which was a violent and pathetic, patriotic declaration of her belief in victory over the Nazis. She had many dramatic experiences during the war, and after the war she started to look for means of expressing those experiences. She gradually found a form somewhat similar to her earlier miniatures, but now much more realistic, relating not to painting and to old poetry but to snapshots. (When reading those poems I sometimes thought about poets of the very beginning of our century, such as the French poet Blaise Cendrars, who published a volume of documentaries originally called *Kodak*.) She made two attempts, I should say. Soon after the war she published a number of such prose poems, snapshots of situations. And then many years later, some thirty years later, she succeeded in writing a cycle of short poems about her experiences as a military nurse in the Warsaw Uprising of 1944, which were published as a volume, *Building the Barricade*. Her poems can be divided into those where she speaks as a persona, speaks about her direct experience, and those which are objective, those which describe things she knows actually happened but where her persona doesn't appear. I guess the reader who has read only poems in our selection would have difficulty in guessing another side of Anna Swir's personality. So it seems appropriate here to read a few of the war poems, first from her initial attempt and then from those poems about the Warsaw Uprising. Here is a quite objective poem, "A Truck," which very naturalistically describes how people were executed in Warsaw and other Polish cities. (The image of that period, popular in the u.s., that horrors were perpetrated only against the Jews, is not correct. Gentile hostages, so-called hostages, were often taken and executed.) "A Truck" is a prose poem.

That street is often busy at night. Bouncing on cobblestones a truck passes, carrying people who stand in a ringing frost, with bare heads and in paper suits. Their hands are bound behind their backs by barbed wire. Their mouths are sealed with plaster.

The escorting soldier with a glimmer of a cigarette in his lips, his rifle at the ready, sweeps gloomily with his eyes the dumb windows and gates of the lifeless city.

He is somewhat sleepy after yesterday's bout of drinking and probably for that reason he does not notice that on the first floor a windowpane flickered in the light of the moon. Someone noiselessly half-opens a window and, standing, makes a sign with his hand to those who ride to their death.

One of them sees him.

So that's an objective situation. Another poem, "A Manhunt," is about the Gestapo, who would come any time, day or night, and arrest people.

146

It was late afternoon. Lights were already lit here and
there in the town and a powdery snowstorm began to
blow in earnest through deserted streets, when somebody
put his hand silently on the door handle.

It did not appear ominous at all and the man who stepped
up to the door holding a sleepy child on his shoulder did
not know that the house was surrounded.

Or there are poems about the ghetto, scenes from its final destruc-
tion after the ghetto uprising, when whole streets were burned, one
after another.

Ghetto: Two Living Children

Screaming ceased long ago on that street. Only the wind
sometimes plays with a torn-out window in which the
remnants of a windowpane still glitter, and carries over
cobblestones feathers from ripped-open eiderdowns.

At times the same wind brings a sudden shout of many
people from far away. Then it happens that from a cross
street two living children walk out unexpectedly. Holding
each other's hands they escape silently through the middle
of a deserted street.

Up to the spot where, hidden behind a street corner
wrapped in mist, a German soldier at a machine gun
watches day and night on the border of the ghetto.

And here is a poem that is more personal, "A Hospital Blanket,"
which we may consider a passage to her cycle of poems from the

Warsaw Uprising. Swir speaks of her situation as a military nurse.

Under that same hospital blanket with which I cover
myself after a sleepless night, four men had died this week.
Four soldiers – I remember their death agony.

I pull myself over to the side less stained with blood and
fall asleep on the corridor floor, next to a civilian who
gasped and rattled there for twenty-four hours, and just
now stopped and stiffened. They have covered him
already.

I fall asleep for a short while, as the sky outside the
window already whitens and the first morning bird has
already sung in the cold. In a moment a nurse will tug
at the sleeve of my uniform.

"Five o'clock, time to take the patient's temperature."

And now two personal poems from the Warsaw Uprising.

When a Soldier is Dying

By the stretcher, on the floor
I knelt close to him,
I kissed his tunic,
I was saying: you are beautiful,
you can give so much happiness,
you don't know yourself how much happiness,
you will live, my beautiful,
my brave boy.

He smiled and he listened,
his eyelids heavier and heavier,
he did not know that such words
are said to a soldier
only when he is dying.

Another poem needs a brief commentary. In a city under constant bombardment and artillery fire, it was very dangerous to cross a few streets.

A Conversation Through the Door

At five in the morning
I knock on his door.
I say through the door:
In the hospital at Sliska Street
your son, a soldier, is dying.

He half-opens the door,
does not remove the chain.
Behind him his wife
shakes.

I say: your son asks his mother
to come.
He says: the mother won't come.
Behind him the wife
shakes.

I say: the doctor allowed us
to give him wine.
He says: please wait.

He hands me a bottle through the door,
locks the door,
locks it with a second key.

Behind the door his wife
begins to scream as if she were in labor.

And here is a poem, "I am Afraid of Fire," where her persona also
speaks. This is a very, very realistic picture because there were
whole streets burning from the shelling. She is running through such
a street. I know very few poems where the presence of fire is so
powerfully felt.

I Am Afraid of Fire

Why am I so afraid
running in the street
that is burning.

After all, there are no people here
only fire buzzing up to the sky
and that crash is not a bomb,
it's only three floors collapsed.

Naked liberated flames dance,
they wave their arms
through the holes of windows.
It's sinful
to spy on
naked flames,
it's sinful to eavesdrop
on the speech of free fire.

I run away from that speech
which resounded on the earth
earlier than the speech of man.

NATHAN: These poems prompt another question – maybe unanswerable. In style, a poem like "Fire" sounds very much like Swir's erotic poems. Why after the war did she so drastically reduce her subject matter almost exclusively to erotic poetry, except for *Building the Barricade*? Did she see the "wars" of sex, of mind and body – stripped of romance and hope – as a sort of measure for all other experience?

MIŁOSZ: That's very hard to answer. However, my impression is that even as a young girl she was of a rather skeptical, ironic nature. Maybe her upbringing helps explain this. As she tells it, she grew up in the workshop of her father, a painter, and she would do her lessons sitting on the floor; she was surrounded with paintings by her father, reproductions of paintings, and easels. And she was very poor, extremely poor. I guess a kind of dry irony found its way into her early poems: stylized, very aesthetic miniatures about art. That was one factor. Another, of course, was the experience of war, but I should draw your attention to one thing which to me is rather strange: she seems to have only one kind of religion, and that is patriotism. Absolute devotion to her country. Patriotism goes together strangely with her dry, ironic outlook. It's very hard to visualize a person who is not only ironic, but also sarcastic about herself and about her body, about really everything, who at the same time recognizes the true value of heroism, of the duty of soldiers. My guess is that a poet may change considerably during his or her lifetime but basic orientations are always there. Of course it may be that the war experiences marked her, but not so that she would become a completely different person.

NATHAN: I didn't make myself too clear. Maybe I can put the question this way: After an experience like the war, why would she choose – or be driven to – a subject that seems so unrelated to war and so deliberately limiting? I can see why war might push an already lean style to an even harsher leanness, but I can't see why it would push her toward a subject so different.

MIŁOSZ: You mean love.

NATHAN: Love.

MIŁOSZ: Well, it's curious that she started to write, or at least to publish, love poems when she was sixty. But these poems, like her war poems, probably had a long history of revisions. Basically, the subject of all her poetry is love and death, two elemental things. And I shouldn't say that her poetry is very rich as it stands now; I should say that it is obsessive, poignant, terse, reduced to a certain narrow range. Why? Perhaps because of the constant effort to be concise, and not to go beyond her capabilities, since if you use a dry pen and you do little drawings, you cannot be a Rembrandt. Rembrandt did little drawings too, but he also did other things.

NATHAN: If she is a miniaturist, it seems to me she is an abstract one. As you say, the situations are filled out with a few strokes, the characters are nameless, the locale anywhere. It's almost geometrical, a matter of line more than color, of form more than substance. And this concentration makes for the peculiar intensity of the poems. This I see, but from where does the patriotism you were speaking of spring? How can her ruthless irreverence about things romantic or religious be squared with her worship of her nation as almost a religious object?

MIŁOSZ: That's a very good question. In Polish literature there is a very strong tradition of Romantic activist poetry; after all, the struggle for independence lasted throughout the whole nineteenth century and endowed the national identity with a sacred aura. There are some poems by Swir in which she speaks of the Polish earth receiving ashes, blood, everything, as though in a religious sacrifice. This devotion is something that unites Polish atheists and Polish believers. Outsiders might ask: Why are Polish churches full? Why are there pilgrimages to the shrine of the so-called Black Madonna in which both believers and non-believers participate? All this could not be reduced to a purely political position against Communist governments. It is, rather, an affirmation of basic values, of the existence of good and evil, a basic attachment to meaning. So Anna Swir is very much in the current tradition. You see, these things may be somewhat difficult for foreigners; it is assumed that the liberated woman, a woman who doesn't make claim to any religious denomination, should be liberated as far as her country is concerned. But that's not true in the case of the Poles.

NATHAN: Isn't it strange, though, that she has one set of poems – exclusively about war – in her closet, another set – mostly about love – on her desk, as if they had no connection? Did she think perhaps that to bring the two subjects together would be somehow to debase the war poems? Other poets – Sappho at the very beginning of our tradition and Amichai today – mix these subjects, using one to illuminate the other. It's strange to me how she compartmentalized these two obsessive subjects, except in the poem about the dying soldier. Is this a legitimate puzzlement on my part?

MIŁOSZ: I'm not sure, because her war poems are not abstract but are always snapshots of a human situation: there is a human being, or a group of human beings, in every poem. And there are a lot of poems about hospitals, civil hospitals after the war, about people terminally ill, about all the women in the hospitals. And there are ferociously feminist poems that are really class-war poems: the males are oppressors, the women are proletarians...terse poems of how women are treated by those brutes, males. So there are bridges.

NATHAN: Is there any Western writer to whom Swir is at all comparable?

MIŁOSZ: None. As I have said already, there were European poets at the very beginning of our century with their passion for reality. Swir wants to touch reality proper; she is, I would say, naturalistic. For me it's very strange because I cannot think of any woman poet in the English language with a similar fierceness in trying to be close to reality. After all, there are many women poets who write about physical love. What do you think?

NATHAN: I was thinking of someone like Sylvia Plath. Readers might say: ah, the connection here is this brutal honesty; but in fact we best know Plath for poems of confession, something Swir doesn't engage in; she's not a confessional poet. It might appear that way when she talks very openly about relations, but you look at the relations and, as we've said, they're almost impersonal. So no, I don't think she's really like American poets. Nor is her work like – the word is "naked" – the naked poetry of a generation back. She's not giving us a glimpse of her "real" life in the sense that American poets are. No, I can't think of anyone who's quite like her.

MIŁOSZ: I cannot find an example in either French poetry or Russian poetry. She stands out as a very peculiar phenomenon.

NATHAN: Nothing in Polish either, no one like her?

MIŁOSZ: I should mention Tadeusz Różewicz, whose poetry is similar. I guess she may have been influenced by him; his poetry has been defined by a critic as "casket-oriented somatism." And it has been said of him that he was marked by his wartime experiences when he was in the Resistance, and since that time a permanent feature of his poetry is a completely desperate view of human beings as flesh that is condemned to die. So she's not alone in this respect.

NATHAN: One more question. Is it possible to divide Polish poets – those writing since or from just before the war – into two classifications? One, a very rough classification: those who were driven by that catastrophe and its aftermath to find a reduced style to match their reduced hopes, and then those who have sought a richer style to – I don't quite know, maybe to find somewhere in experience – the meanings lost in the war? Is this too simple a division and is it particularly Polish?

MIŁOSZ: No; it seems to me, Leonard, that we have here the general problem of world literature, the problem of basic existential despair, and the person who comes to my mind is Samuel Beckett. Undoubtedly poetry like that of Anna Swir or Różewicz is in some respects of that general existential mold. Of course, Swir and Różewicz went through certain war experiences, and that's an excellent bridge to reach that road. But Samuel Beckett didn't go through such things, and he took that road. I don't know, I wouldn't like to be too ponderous and overburden Anna Swir with too much of a philosophical load, but we have to confront the issue, namely that we live in a very peculiar historical period. Life after death was a very strong ingredient of our civilization for many centuries; images of heaven and hell were with us for millennia. The question of salvation and damnation today may be dealt with by people who are religious believers and those who are not believers, but even the believers do not have any images of paradise or hell. Perhaps people who died for Khomeini had a vision of traditional Muslim paradise, but that was a peculiar situation. And that's why body, diet, vitamins, hospitals, and medicine in general are so much the center of our attention.

NATHAN: That leaves us with this world and no other.

MIŁOSZ: Maybe that would be going too far. Even for Anna Swir. Yet Anna Swir presents a serious challenge not so much to belief as to the images of belief. Think of *The Divine Comedy* and the presence of the other world in it. Personally, I feel the dead are present and part of our lives but, being a modern poet, I am unable to put them in any imaginary space. And for poetry – now we discuss not religion but poetry, which uses images – it's very important isn't it?

Postscript

As this dialogue took place a couple of years ago, I feel I should add a few words. Since then, Anna Swir's position in her country has undergone a change and I am proud to say that my articles in Poland's literary press about her oeuvre have contributed to its re-evaluation. There had been an earlier tendency to encapsulate her work in the category of Feminist poetry, and in that way to dismiss her fierceness. She is now regarded as a truly eminent poet of metaphysical orientation, which links her to some of the the Baroque poets, obsessed with the perishability of the flesh.

What Leonard Nathan and I have said in our dialogue is valid, yet my formulations now seem to me a little too far on the bleak side. Opening myself to her verses, I have been more and more conquered by her extraordinary, powerful, exuberant, and joyous personality. Reading her was like discovering in someone who is close to us an unsuspected, strange and admirable being. Perhaps I was even falling in love with her. What I found particularly attractive in her was her calm in accepting reality, whether it brought bliss or suffering. A mood of detachment is visible in her late poems on light and silence – also in her short poems about the pleasures of manual work. To have met such a person through her poems has inclined me to faith and optimism.

Wisdom of acceptance was once called submission to the Divine Will. For Frederic Nietzsche it took the form of *amor fati*, love of fate. Whatever term we use, Anna met her last ordeal if an incurable illness just as she had previously met war and love: bravely. We decided to end this volume with a poem she wrote in the hospital before the operation. According to her daughter, she made peace with the Roman Catholic church while on her deathbed. In her later poems it was apparent that she had been gradually moving towards a supreme quietude.

Tomorrow They Will Carve Me

Death came and stood by me.
I said: I am ready.
I am lying in the surgery clinic in Kraków.
Tomorrow
they will carve me.

There is much strength in me. I can live,
can run, dance, and sing.
All that is in me, but if neccessary
I will go.

Today
I make account of my life.
I was a sinner,
I was beating my head against earth,
I implored from the earth and the sky
forgiveness.

I was pretty and ugly,
wise and stupid,
very happy and very unhappy
often I had wings
and would float in air.

I trod a thousand paths in the sun and in snow,
I danced with my friend under the stars.

I saw love
in many human eyes,
I ate with delight
my slice of happiness.

Now I am lying in the surgery clinic in Kraków.
It stands by me.
Tomorrow
they will carve me.
Through the window the trees of May, beautiful like life,
and in me, humility, fear, and peace.

CzesŁaw MiŁosz was born in Lithuania in 1911 and lived in Poland until 1951, when he was granted asylum in France. The author of dozens of books, including the poetry books *Facing the River* (Ecco Press, 1995) and *Collected Poems* (Ecco Press, 1988), as well as the prose volumes *A Year of a Hunter* (Farrar, Straus & Giroux, 1984) and *Beginning with My Streets* (Farrar, Straus & Giroux, 1992), he was awarded the Nobel Prize for Literature in 1980. Since 1960 he has lived in Berkeley, California.

Leonard Nathan is the author of nine volumes of poetry, including *Returning Your Call*, which was nominated for the National Book Award. The recipient of a Guggenheim Award, the National Institute of Arts and Letters prize for poetry, and many other awards and honors, he is an avid birdwatcher whose book on the subject *Diary of a Left-Handed Birdwatcher* is due to be published by Graywolf Press in October, 1996. He lives in Kensington, California.

Book design and composition by John D. Berry. The text type is Sabon, designed in 1966 by Jan Tschichold, and the display type is American Garamond italic. Sabon is based on the 16th-century types of Claude Garamond, and was designed as a functional and elegant text type that could be used simultaneously in hot metal on Monotype and Linotype typesetting machines and for hand-setting in metal foundry type. This is Linotype's digitized version of the typeface. American Garamond is Bitstream's version of Linotype's Garamond No. 3, which is also based on the types of Claude Garamond, but as interpreted in the 17th century by Jean Jannon.

Printed in the USA
CPSIA information can be obtained
at www.ICGtesting.com
JSHW020136280823
47300JS00001B/2